W9-CDX-919

MARS

by Charnan Simon

21st Century Junior Library

CHERRY LAKE PUBLISHING * ANN ARBOR, MICHIGAN

Published in the United States of America by Cherry Lake Publishing
Ann Arbor, Michigan
www.cherrylakepublishing.com

Content Adviser: Dr. Tobias Owen, University of Hawaii Institute for Astronomy

Photo Credits: Cover, ©Orlando Florin Rosu/Dreamstime.com; cover and pages 6, 12, 16, 18, and 20, ©NASA; page 4, ©iStockphoto.com/JoeLena; page 8, ©ostill/Shutterstock, Inc.; page 10, ©iStockphoto.com/larslentz; page 14, ©Aaron Rutten/Dreamstime.com

LIBRARY OF CONGRESS CATALOGING-IN-PUBLICATION DATA

Simon, Charnan.
Mars/by Charnan Simon.
   p. cm.—(21st junior library)
Includes bibliographical references and index.
ISBN-13: 978-1-61080-082-2 (lib. bdg.)
ISBN-10: 1-61080-082-6 (lib. bdg.)
1. Mars (Planet)—Juvenile literature. I. Title. II. Series.
QB641.S4935 2011
523.43—dc22   2010052191

Cherry Lake Publishing would like to acknowledge the work of The Partnership for 21st Century Skills. Please visit www.21stcenturyskills.org for more information.

Printed in the United States of America
Corporate Graphics Inc.
July 2011
CLFA09

CONTENTS

Mars is the planet closest to Earth.

Our Neighbor in Space

Mars is one of the eight planets in our **solar system**. All eight planets travel around the Sun. Mars is smaller and colder than our own planet, Earth.

Think!

Earth is the third planet from the Sun. Mars is the fourth planet from the Sun. Do you think this explains why Mars is colder than Earth? How?

Almost all of Mars' surface is covered with red soil.

The Red Planet

You can see Mars from your backyard on some nights. You don't even need a **telescope**! Mars glows like a bright reddish orange dot in the night sky. It looks red because of all the **iron** in its soil.

Ask your parents or teacher why iron makes Mars look red. Have you ever seen rusty iron? What color is it? What makes it turn rusty? What might this tell you about Mars?

7

The god Mars was thought to protect Rome's army during battles.

The **ancient Romans** gave Mars its name. They named it after their god of war. They thought the planet's red color was like the color of blood. This bloody color reminded them of war. People have called the planet Mars ever since then.

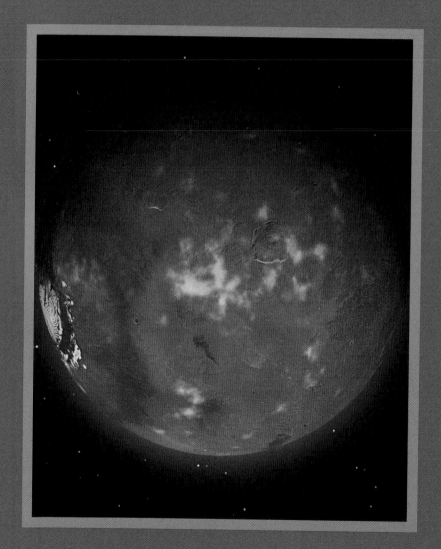

The area around Mars' north pole is covered in ice.

What Does Mars Look Like?

Mars is a cold, dry planet. There are clouds on Mars, but it never rains. **Scientists** think Mars once had rivers, lakes, and even oceans. Today, all water on Mars is frozen. Mars has huge fields of underground ice at its north and south poles.

Plains cover much of Mars' surface.

12

Mars has deep **canyons** and wide **plains**. Windstorms blow red dust over the planet's surface.

Some places on Mars were formed long ago when floods rushed over the land. Other places might be dried-up riverbeds. But there is no flowing water on Mars today.

Mars' moons are very small compared to Earth's Moon.

14

Mars also has the largest **volcanoes** in the solar system! These volcanoes are much bigger than the tallest mountains on Earth.

Mars has two small moons named Phobos and Deimos. They go around Mars just as our Moon goes around Earth.

Create!

What do you think Mars looks like? Draw your own picture of the canyons, plains, and volcanoes on Mars.

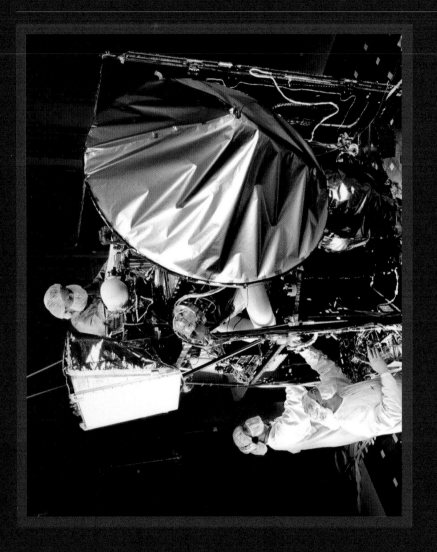

This device was sent to Mars in 1998 to get information about the planet's weather.

How Do We Know About Mars?

People have never visited Mars. Scientists use telescopes to study it. Many of these telescopes are right here on Earth. Others are attached to spaceships that fly near Mars. The spaceships take pictures and send them back to Earth.

Rovers are built to go over all kinds of rocks and hills. This rover is being tested on Earth.

Some spaceships have even landed on Mars. These spaceships carried special robots called **rovers**.

Rovers roll around the planet collecting information. They also take pictures. They use radio signals to send the information back to scientists on Earth.

Pictures from rovers help scientists learn what Mars' surface looks like.

You may have seen movies about aliens from Mars. These are just stories. There are probably no living things at all on Mars. If there are, they would be too small to see without a **microscope**.

There are rovers with names such as Spirit and Opportunity on Mars. They help us discover exciting new things about our neighbor in space!

Make a Guess!

Could people survive on Mars? What would we need to spend time on the red planet? Remember that it is very cold. How would we breathe?

GLOSSARY

ancient Romans (AYN-shunt ROH-muhnz) people who lived long ago in Rome or in places ruled by Rome

canyons (KAN-yuhnz) narrow valleys with high, steep sides

iron (EYE-urn) a kind of very hard metal

microscope (MYE-kro-skohp) a tool used to look at very small objects

plains (PLAYNZ) large, flat areas of land

rovers (RO-verz) wheeled robots used to collect information on other planets

scientists (SYE-uhn-tists) people who study nature and make discoveries

solar system (SOH-lur SISS-tuhm) a star, such as the Sun, and all the planets and moons that move around it

telescope (TEL-uh-skope) a tool used to look at faraway objects

volcanoes (vol-KAY-nohz) mountains that throw out smoke, lava, and ashes from vents in the top

FIND OUT MORE

BOOKS

James, Lincoln. *Mars: The Red Planet.* New York: Gareth Stevens Publishing, 2011.

Loewen, Nancy. *Seeing Red: The Planet Mars.* Minneapolis: Picture Window Books, 2008.

Orme, Helen, and David Orme. *Let's Explore Mars.* Milwaukee: Gareth Stevens Publishing, 2007.

WEB SITES

ESA Kids—Our Universe
www.esa.int/esaKIDSen/ SEM3L6WJD1E_OurUniverse_0.html
Learn more about the surface of Mars and its two moons.

Mars Exploration Program—Mars for Kids
marsprogram.jpl.nasa.gov/ participate/funzone/
Keep up with the latest Mars information from NASA on this fun interactive site.

Phoenix Mars Mission— Just for Kids
phoenix.lpl.arizona.edu/kids.php
Enjoy fun activities and pictures that will help you learn more about Mars.

INDEX

C
canyons, 13
clouds, 11
color, 7, 9, 13

D
Deimos (moon), 15
dust, 13

I
ice, 11
iron, 7

L
location, 5

M
Mars (Roman god), 9
moons, 15

N
name, 9
north pole, 11

P
Phobos (moon), 15
pictures, 17, 19
plains, 13

R
rovers, 19, 21

S
scientists, 11, 17, 19
size, 5
solar system, 5, 15
south pole, 11

spaceships, 17, 19
Sun, 5
surface, 13, 15, 19

T
telescopes, 17
temperature, 5

V
volcanoes, 15

W
water, 11, 13
windstorms, 13

ABOUT THE AUTHOR

Charnan Simon is a former editor of *Cricket, Click,* and *Spider* magazines. She has written more than 100 books for young readers and loves looking up at the night sky. Before she wrote this book, she didn't know that the moons of Mars are named Phobos and Deimos.